Blackpool North Pier

by
Juliette W Gregson

All Rights Reserved. Copyright © 2014 Juliette W Gregson

No part of this book may be reproduced or transmitted in any form or by any means, graphic, electronic, or mechanical, including photocopying, recording, taping or by any information storage or retrieval system, without the permission in writing from the publisher.

Juliette Gregson

ACKNOWLEDGEMENTS

I am indebted to all the kind people that have helped me achieve a goal that I have held for a very long time, to produce a local history and heritage book that reflects my passion for the town of Blackpool.

Many thanks to David & Kath Gregson (thank you for the love and inspiration from you both); my late grandparents Frank & Elsie Gregson who always took me on little jaunts about the town pointing out places of interest; Nick Moore; Steve Gomersall; Martyn King; Matthew Corbett; Graham Coleman; Peter and Sue Sedgwick for letting me capture such an iconic piece of Blackpool History; Stephen Mercer for just being 'fabulous'; Andi Musson; Roy Thomson; Pete Skinner; Peter Lindup; John Burke; Tony Sharkey for the Local & Family History Centre, Blackpool Central Library collection; Ian McLoughlin; Nick Entwistle; Paul Rodgers; Barry J Barnes; Barry McCann; Dr Chris Lee; Christo Cunliffe-Gregson; Kate Yates; Joanne M S McDonnell; Brian Hughes and Michelle Harris. Any omissions and mistakes are mine.

Special thanks to Paul Galley for the lovely introduction, and finally the wonderful and now, alas, late Phil Barker who made my journey so much easier with his exquisite collection of postcards and memorabilia.

I would like to dedicate this book to my phenomenal partner Anthony Cunliffe who, without any shadow of doubt, made my journey much easier with his words of inspiration, encouragement and unwavering support.

Juliette Gregson

Juliette Gregson

INTRODUCTION *by Councillor Paul Galley*

Just like the famous Tower, North Pier is one of the most recognisable landmarks in Blackpool. The endearing, Victorian structure attracts visitors and residents alike and is as much a vital element of Blackpool as the famous trams and Tower. Three generations of my family since the 1920's have enjoyed the North Pier, from relaxing on its promenade to spending time in the amusement arcade and theatre.

The North Pier, like my family and society itself, has changed immensely during that time, but has always retained its unique qualities of being a quieter more reflective place compared to Blackpool's other two piers.

It's that uniqueness which makes the North Pier and Blackpool itself such a special place, and why I decided to move to the town in 2010.

Whilst to a stranger, on first glance, the North Pier is just one of three piers in the town, for many, however, it's a rich wonderful place, with a history worthy of a Hollywood blockbuster with fire, shipwrecks, entertainers and politicians along with memories of so many enjoyed holidays and day trips.

For me, though, alongside all of it's rich history, it shouts to us all the sort of place Blackpool was, and will be again – a place that lives to the town's motto of "Progress", utilising the skills of Eugenius Birch so well it will one day be drawn on again to make Blackpool one of the most incredible places in the UK where everything is possible and our dreams and ambitions have no limitations.

The timing of this wonderful book could not be better, with the North Pier having new owners, the wonderful and gifted Sedgwick family – a family whose history is as rich and as successful as the pier itself. They are a family who understand how piers and entertainment work. The Sedgwicks, have, in the short time they have owned the pier, refurbished large parts of it, including parts of its theatre as well as commencing work on restoring the structure of the pier of itself.

The fruits of that hard work are already beginning to bear fruit with news that shows at the pier are being extended due to popular demand.

With the Pier in safe hands, exciting times lie ahead for it and along with its rich history, North Pier is something we can all be proud of, and continue to be proud of into the future.

Juliette in writing this book has brought all of her experience as a resort-based specialist heritage photographer and social historian to the fore and her love for the North Pier and Blackpool, its rich past and even richer future shines through every enjoyable page.

Enjoy this great book and let it be your guide to the pier we have today and use it as a guide to the pier we will have tomorrow.

Cllr Paul Galley (Blackpool Councillor)

BLACKPOOL NORTH PIER

(Photograph Antony Cutler)

Above is a rare image of one the Blackpool Pier Company £5 share certificates.

This one was bought by a Thornton Littlewood Esq. of Rochdale.

This had led on from the original concept when, in 1861, a group of the town's most prominent movers and shakers had gathered in the Clifton Arms Hotel to discuss the idea of building a Pier where the most 'in vogue' Victorians could exercise in the pastime of promenading in the open air.

(Photograph courtesy of Local & Family History Centre, Blackpool Central Library.)

A captivating image that shows the original design by Eugenius Birch who was most acclaimed for his seaside pier constructions.

During his life he was responsible for no fewer than fourteen of them, including some of the best known such as Brighton West & of course Blackpool North Pier.

Most piers of the era were made using cast iron.

Birch thought that if wrought iron was to be used it would take a lot of repairing if the pier were to be damaged.

It is noted that now due to disregardance of heritage very little remains of his pioneering work.

(Photograph Phil Barker)

An etching of the opening ceremony, May 21st 1863.

Dignitaries that attended included the voluntary artillery, deputations of freemasons & oddfellows, the trades of Blackpool, ancient order of druids (with two high priests in full costume and a bard mounted on an ass) bathing vans, hackney carriages and of course a chimney sweep.

(Photograph and information Phil Barker)

A medallion was made to commemorate the opening of the Pier in 1863 showing the new pier.

On the reverse is: "The first pile was screwed June 21st 1862 – opened to the public May 21st 1863 – length 1350 feet, breadth 21 feet."

The medal itself was made of white metal and was 31 mm in diameter.

Many medallions were made to also celebrate other major events or buildings, such as the Blackpool Tower (stating that a foundation stone was laid September 25th, 1891); one for Blackpool Winter Gardens of July, 1878; the erection of Blackpool Big Wheel in 1896, and its subsequent 1926 dismantling; and, in 1911, one of the coronation of King George V and his consort Queen Mary.

Blackpool also had the edge in souvenirs as medals were made from copper salvaged from Nelson's Flagship HMS Foudroyant in 1897. (More on the story of the shipwreck later.)

(Photograph Phil Barker)

An etching from the Illustrated London News of 1863.

It was said that over 20,000 people had descended on the town to join in the jubilant festivities.

Major Francis Preston used his cannon to officially open the new pier.

Talbot Square and the surrounding area were strewn with banners, flags and bunting, while a band played the specially composed tune of 'The Blackpool Pier Polka'.

(Photograph Phil Barker. Other information Cyril Critchlow Collection - courtesy of Local & Family History Centre, Blackpool Central Library)

Another etching showing a more different viewpoint looking towards Talbot Square from the Pier. On the top left can be seen the bell tower of the Sacred Heart Church, which was founded by the Jesuits as the town's first Roman Catholic church, being built in 1857 to a design by Edward Welby Pugin. To the right of the picture is the hotel known as the Clifton Arms (formally known as Forshaws and now, in 2013, operating as a travel lodge). Forshaws was one of four hotels that were built in the late 1700's as Blackpool was emerging as a seaside resort. It is also noted that after the opening ceremony the dignitaries attended a meal that included the directors, shareholders and guests that also included Mr E Birch and his family and Mr Laidlow, the contractor of the works. The Laidlaws began in the early nineteenth century as brass founders and Venetian blind makers at Simon Square Edinburgh, and manufactured all of the ornate ironwork used in the construction of many early Victorian pleasure piers around our coasts. The few surviving structures are at Hastings, Brighton West Pier and Blackpool North.

(Photograph Phil Barker)

An early 1863 image that shows a lone man admiring the view out to the Irish Sea, and to the far right a family perhaps also looking at the delights that North Pier can provide.

Victorians loved new 'innovations' and the pier enabled the 'well at heel' gentry to walk close to and over the sea without fear or danger.

In 1866 the British Government concurred that a second pier would be allowed to be built.

Objections from the Blackpool Pier Company arose stating that it would be too close to their own.

(Photograph Juliette W Gregson – own collection)

As sanctioned by parliamentary order, a landing jetty was allowed to be built at the end of North Pier by additional stages between 1864 and 1867.

The Blackpool Pier Company used the jetty to operate pleasure steamers and boats that made various trips to the surrounding areas.

Steamers such as "Queen of the Bay" & "Clifton" began to cruise.

This image is one of the "Clifton".

(Photograph Phil Barker)

Living on the coast of a seaside town we are, of course, prone to violent gales and storms of epic proportions created by the Irish Sea.

Looking through the history of Blackpool, throughout the ages land, houses and cattle have been engulfed by the barbaric nature of the weather.

In the distance that can be seen from the North Pier is the Hotel Metropole. In 1776 a Lawrence Bailey (farmer) from the Layton area of Blackpool set to build a hotel by the immediate seashore hence the original name of 'Baileys'.

It is interesting to note that this hotel is still the only one that sits on the shoreline of the promenade.

THE FAST SALOON P.S. "GREYHOUND". DAILY FROM NORTH PIER—BLACKPOOL.

(Photograph Phil Barker)

The Greyhound was built in 1895 for the North Pier Steamship Company and was later passed onto the Blackpool Passenger Steamboat Company (which was on Birley Street and registered in 1894).

This steamer ran from Blackpool to Llandudno and the delightful Isle of Man.

After the First World War the 'Greyhound' was no longer making money and was sold off, before finally going to Turkey and being renamed as 'Buyuk Ada'.

THE SALOON, P.S. "GREYHOUND". — BLACKPOOL.

(Photograph Phil Barker)

    As can be seen in this postcard, the luxury of the Greyhound was quite apparent with the opulence of the furnishings.
    I would suspect that paying passengers who had never used a steamer before would have been delighted by the visual display of the North West coastline and by the sumptuousness of the interior.

NORTH PIER
STEAMSHIP COMPANY (BLACKPOOL) LIMITED.

The New, Fast and Powerful SALOON STEAMER—

"GREYHOUND,"

Especially designed and built by Messrs. JAMES & GEORGE THOMPSON LIMITED of Clydebank, for this Company to run between Blackpool and the Isle of Man, together with the

"BELLE" and "CLIFTON,"

And other Steamers will Sail Daily during the Season (weather and other circumstances permitting) to

Douglas (Isle of Man).
Llandudno (North Wales).
Liverpool.
Southport.

Also from SOUTHPORT (Daily), MORECAMBE TOWN, and BARROW (for Furness Abbey), WINDERMERE, BOWNESS, AMBLESIDE, And Daily Cruises out to MORECAMBE BAY, &c.

For Particulars see Times at the Blackpool North Pier and Southport Pier Entrances.

J. H. ROBINSON, Secretary,
TALBOT CHAMBERS, BLACKPOOL.

(Photograph Phil Barker)

An advert showing the trips that North Pier ran, including 'Belle' (originally known as Llandudno Belle) that wasn't profitable in her native Wales.

Also shown are the destinations to others places of interest that Victorian visitors may have wanted to venture to and see the sights.

> **POINTS ABOUT THE PIERS**
>
> "At the piers there is plenty of amusement in its most attractive form." — BELFAST WEEKLY TELEGRAPH.
>
> the Piers, where all can enjoy "moonbeam, and sunbeam, and song," take no low rank among the pleasures, and have no small share in the business of the day.
>
> The initial function of Piers is, however, to enable people to embark upon or land from boats. This is sometimes forgotten. But reminders are often forthcoming at Blackpool, whence pleasure steamers galore start daily from the North and Central Piers on extended trips to a variety of destinations. The property of the Blackpool Passenger Steamboat Company, the vessels are specially fitted for the requirements of the service, their arrangements being excellent and their appointments luxurious, while in speed and stability they leave nothing to be desired. Eminently comfortable, to boot, they are deservedly popular, and have contributed to make Blackpool the recognised centre from which to visit other watering-places, more or less adjacent, a course presenting obvious advantages to the sightseer, who is thus enabled to survey the chief points on the coast with the smallest amount of trouble and the least expenditure of time.
>
> On the other hand, most of the localities thus made accessible by sea are without similar means of communication with Blackpool and with the other places in the list.
>
> The advantages of Blackpool, as a base, are consequently apparent. A table of trips, fares, and times is herewith appended:—
>
> | | 1st Class s. d. | 2nd Class s. d. | Distance Miles | Voyage about | | 1st Class s. d. | 2nd Class s. d. | Distance Miles | Voyage about |
> |---|---|---|---|---|---|---|---|---|---|
> | Douglas, I.O.M. | 4 6 | 3 0 | 63 | 3½ hrs. | Southport | 3 3 | 2 3 | 16 | 1½ hrs. |
> | Llandudno | 4 6 | 3 0 | 46 | 2½ „ | Liverpool | 3 6 | 2 6 | 35 | 2 „ |
> | Beaumaris | 4 6 | 3 0 | 58 | 3½ „ | Morecambe | 3 6 | 2 6 | 22 | 1½ „ |
> | Bangor | 4 6 | 3 0 | 60 | 3½ „ | *Fleetwood | 2 0 | 1 6 | 13 | 1 „ |
> | Menai Bridge | 4 6 | 3 0 | 61 | 3½ „ | | | | | |
>
> * To return by rail or electric car.
>
> These Fares include all Pier Tolls.

(Photograph Phil Barker)

This postcard describes the delights and original function of the Pier(s) and, of course, the virtues of taking a trip to another 'watering hole'!

All classes were catered to with the pocket, as can be seen by the variety of the fares on offer.

(Photograph Phil Barker)

I believe that this is an early postcard of the 'Belle', which shows a side view of the steamer.

It also seems that this ship was not as popular as others in the fleet, with the lack of having no saloon for the paying gentry and a very small deck for the ladies and gentlemen to view and parade.

(Photograph Phil Barker)

This postcard with an unknown steamer in the background is pre-1923 as the second Cenotaph War Memorial has not yet replaced the temporary one that was in front of the Metropole Hotel.

The plaques were by Gilbert Ledward best known as being chosen as the sculptor commissioned to produce The Guards Memorial.

The new inscription read: '*In Memory of Our Glorious Dead, 1914-1918, 1939-1945*'.

Pleasure Steamers, Blackpool.

(Photograph Phil Barker)

The Palace Theatre, to the left in the background, was built on the site of a former theatre called the 'Prince of Wales', later housing swimming baths (hall of aquatic variety entertainment).

The Alhambra lost money and was sold to the 'Blackpool Tower Company' and renamed as the 'Palace'.

To the right of the Tower we can just see the Royal Hotel & Market. In later images we will be able to see that this is the site of an iconic art deco designed 'Woolworths'.

(Photograph Ian McLoughlin Collection)

Ian McLoughlin kindly provided this fantastic image from his own collection.

It shows the beach in front of Blackpool Tower in possibly the 1930's.

I love the way it illustrates how life moved at a gentler place back then!

(Photograph Ian McLoughlin Collection)

From Ian's collection again, precise date unknown but guessed to be around the 1930 period.

This delightful image shows the beach with two lone paddlers at high tide, perhaps watching the steamer coming into the jetty.

Blackpool North Pier

(Photograph Phil Barker)

A delightful postcard dated about the 1900's that was available for the passengers to buy and send back to relatives to show what a great time was to be had in Blackpool.

It also shows how busy the 'Greyhound' was on the trips around the Fylde coast and further that ran from the North Pier.

(Photo Juliette W Gregson – own collection)

From around the 1920's, an unknown steamer that seems to have disembarking passengers from a trip on the Irish Sea.

On the right hand side is another steamer that seems to be waiting for the day trippers to board and see the wonderful scenery that the Blackpool coast and surrounding areas have to offer.

(Photograph Juliette W Gregson – own collection)

This postcard from 1929 shows the Tynwald – an iron packet steamer (the third vessel to have that name), which was used by the Isle of Man Steam Packet Company.

On returning to normal service after the Great War, as we can see in this image, she was very popular with excursion trips to Blackpool.

(Photograph Juliette W Gregson – own collection)

This image is dated from 1882, and shows the paddle steamers crowded to excess on the North Pier jetty.

The two steamers in question on the photograph are the ex-Mersey tug, 'Great Britain' and also the Morecambe Steamboat Company, 'Roses'.

In the background you can see how busy the jetty is with waiting passengers.

(Photograph Ian McLoughlin Collection)

Unknown date, but this image is a great example of how rough the Irish Sea could get on our Blackpool coastline.

Taken from the upper pier, this photograph shows the ferocity and power that English weather can create on our Fylde shores.

Even now in 2014 over the past year we have seen what the force of nature can do to the Blackpool coastline.

(Photograph courtesy of Local & Family History Centre, Blackpool Central Library)

A lone man in a smart bowler hat looking out to sea and admiring the quiet North Pier. In the foreground we can see how sparse the Pier was before more buildings were added and in the distance we can see the original Pavilion before it was destroyed by fire.

(Photograph courtesy of Local & Family History Centre, Blackpool Central Library)

The band stand from 1875.

To the left you can just make out the tea room that catered for the visitors on the day.

You can also see the lovely ladies in their Sunday best promenading along with sunshades to protect their skin. How much that has changed in today's century!

It is also interesting to see the gentlemen in full suits on what could have only been a hot summer day.

(Photograph courtesy of Local & Family History Centre, Blackpool Central Library)

In the background we can see one of the popular steamers coming alongside the jetty to perhaps drop off or pick up passengers.

To the left you can see the delightful Indian Pavilion inspired by the Hindu Temple of Binderabund, which carried the inscription 'the hearing falls in love before vision.'

(Photograph courtesy of Local & Family History Centre, Blackpool Central Library)

'Promenaders please keep to the right' is the small sign you can see attached to the 'fancy bazaar', which the ladies and gents of that day seem to be doing.

In the shop is a clearance sale that is going on, which is selling off pictures of the pier and steamboats.

In one of the windows are some fans, which the ladies may have wished to use whilst walking along or perhaps a present for a loved one back home.

(Photograph Juliette W Gregson – own collection)

A postcard pre-1928 (before the Big Wheel was dismantled) taken from the Indian pavilion.

It's interesting to note how as the years progress we can see the changing skyline of Blackpool Promenade. No longer can we see the Big Wheel, to the left of the Tower the Woolworths building also has not been built.

We can just see the top of the dome of the Winter Gardens though.

(Photograph Juliette W Gregson – own collection)

Interior shot of the first Indian Pavilion.

In 1877 North Pier's extensions – the Indian Pavilion and the two wings – were officially opened on the 20th of June.

The Pavilion became renowned for elegant and refined concerts.

Famous and noted conductors of the day included Edward de Jong, Signor Rossegari and Simon Speelman.

(Photograph Phil Barker)

The original Pavilion was built after the opening of the North Pier itself (1874).

The design and construction was entrusted to Richard Knill Freeman, (although the dates are open to debate with his possible involvement) whose work included churches, schools and vicarages.

However Freeman was involved in other Blackpool buildings that included Central Pier, Holy Trinity Church and Blackpool South Shore Hydro.

(Photograph Ian McLoughlin Collection)

One could discuss that good weather is paramount to having a good holiday in a seaside town.

Ian's photograph from *circa* 1930's, shows that the Blackpool holidaymakers who came to the area still knew how to have a good time even when the weather was frightful!

This photograph also shows the old sea walls before the promenade was renovated.

Wreck of the Sirene at Blackpool, Oct. 9th, 1892 – immediately after damaging the Pier.

(Photograph Phil Barker)

In October 1892 the 'Sirene' had been sailing from the port of Fleetwood and was captured by the gales of the Fylde coast.

Due to the atrocious weather the 667 ton vessel smashed and destroyed some of the North Pier decking near to the sea wall.

The force of the boat crash also wrecked shops and the arcade.

Amazingly the eleven crewmembers managed to climb onto the pier and walk to the promenade and safety.

(Photograph Phil Barker)

This photograph shows after the weather had abated how close the 'Sirene' actually was to the North Pier and the extent of the damage that the storm had caused to the vessel and the pier itself.

The Promenade is full of 'sightseers' that have come to gawp at the wreck and see the devastation that it has left, and possibly a few cheeky members of the public may have helped themselves to the odd souvenir or two!

(Photograph Phil Barker)

The tide, now having rescinded, shows the general population having a closer look at the 'Sirene'.

With no Health and Safety officialdom to say 'actually you're too close!', many took the opportunity to see the wreck of the Norwegian vessel that had been built in Sestri Ponente 1867.

Its original route was to have been to the United States of America, but alas it was not to be.

(Photograph Phil Barker)

A little known fact is that, if a ship was wrecked in days gone by, the Captain or master of the ship was usually requested to appear to a Justice of the Peace or Receiver of the Wreck.

Reading deeper into maritime records we discover that it was a W & NW gale blowing with great force that caused the 'Sirene' to lose her rudder and become un-seaworthy, thus causing her to drift and eventual crash into the structure of the North Pier.

(Photograph Juliette W Gregson – own collection)

A vintage plate that is over 100 years old that showed the sort of souvenir that was available to the visitors that came to Blackpool to visit the North Pier.

The detail of the time shows the delightful structure that was available to promenade along come rain or shine.

(Photograph Juliette W Gregson – own collection)

Blackpool has many historic buildings that celebrate the best examples of Victorian architecture.

They are celebrated with 'Blue Plaques' around the town.

Here to the right of North Pier looking towards the Irish Sea is an example of such.

It gives a potted history of the 'Foudroyant', a former flagship of Admiral Lord Nelson.

(Photograph Phil Barker)

When the Foudroyant (second to bear the navel name) was launched in Plymouth in 1798 this was to become Lord Nelson's flagship for the next two years.

English oak was used in her construction and some of this lovely panelling can still be found at Blackpool Football Club.

When the Foudroyant was no longer needed for service, for many years, after great repairs and nearly being sold for salvage, she was to travel around as a tourist attraction and came to Blackpool.

The Foudroyant was anchored between Central and the North Pier and had many of the steamers take pleasure trips out to her.

(Photograph by Phil Barker)

On June 15th the weather began to change still with people on board.

As the night progressed into the early morning the storm raged about the Foudroyant that caused the anchor to fail.

The masts broke and later on the ship deck also broke. Luckily the vessel missed the North Pier and ended up just past what we know as Cocker Square.

The remaining 28 members of the crew were eventually saved by the Blackpool lifeboat 'Samuel Fletcher'.

(Photograph by Phil Barker)

True to Blackpool form, the salvage company involved was to receive money if the vessel could be refloated.

If not they could buy the wreck.

This was not to be the case so the company got back some of the initial outlay by making souvenirs from the timber and copper and selling them on to the general public.

Some of the items included furniture, medallions and shown here coins. (Photograph by Phil Barker)

Nelson's flagship, Foudroyant.

(Photograph by Phil Barker)

A wrecked Foudroyant after the crewmembers had been saved by the Samuel Fletcher.

In later years the Samuel Fletcher was kept in Bispham by the Blackpool Sea cadets and had been renovated by the Civic Trust and used on Blackpool's Stanley Park Lake in years gone by.

Now this historic boat is in danger of being lost, as funding is needed to restore it before if has gone beyond being salvaged.

(Photograph Juliette W Gregson – own collection)

My family at one time or another have been members of Masonic lodges.

On occasion we have attended 'Ladies and Gentlemen evenings' and enjoyed a meal in the hall provided. Imagine my delight to find that this chair had Foudroyant history.

Clifton Masonic lodge recorded that two chairs that had been recovered from the Foudroyant were to be donated to the Masonic Hall in Blackpool. Here is one that is used by the 'Worshipful Master' at such events.

(Photograph by Phil Barker)

A delightful example of a Foudroyant souvenir that was owned by Phil Barker.

The cane or walking stick would have been made using the wood salvaged from the wreck, and the 'top' using the copper.

If only the 'item' could talk, what tales would be presented!

> This old beam now carefully preserved, is a relic of the FOUDROYANT, one time Lord Nelson's flagship. After the shipwreck in 1897 the beam was used for many years to support the roof of the Old Smithy previously standing on this site.

(Photograph Juliette W Gregson – own collection)

The 'Old Smithy' in question is now where the Fleetwood Museum Trust is situated

The Museum occupies the old Custom House, built in 1838 and designed by the famous architect Decimus Burton.

Its exhibits trace Fleetwood from past to present – the cargo trade, the fishing industry, passenger services and as a holiday destination that also includes Blackpool.

(Photograph Phil Barker)

Fire swept through the Indian Pavilion on the North Pier on September 11th 1921, causing an extensive amount of damage to the structure as can be seen in the photograph.

The fire was so fierce that all the instruments of the Pier orchestra were destroyed in the blaze as well.

The Pavilion at the time before the devastation could hold up to 2, 500 people when full.

(Photograph Phil Barker)

The Fire Brigade attempted to 'cut off' the Pavilion theatre and had to remove the wooden decking.

If they had not the danger of the flames would have destroyed all of the North Pier.

In this image you can see the extent and ferocity of the damage that the fire inflicted.

The afternoon visitors had only just left after the show had finished so were very lucky not to be caught inside.

(Photograph Phil Barker)

Taken from the jetty this photograph shows the extent again of damage that had been caused.

The total damage caused was thought to have run past £40,000.

In less than an hour the Pavilion itself had dropped into the sea, being watching by the ever-increasing crowds that had come to view the dreadful spectacle that a fire can cause.

(Photograph by Phil Barker)

Another shot of the damage done by fire.

After the event the time taken to repair and rebuild the damaged areas ran to three years.

Only with the quick thinking of the fire brigade was the rest of the North Pier saved.

What is amazing again is the health and safety aspect, as can be seen how close some of the public are standing to watch.

(Photograph Phil Barker)

A scene from the Promenade, possibly just past Blackpool Tower, showing the loss of the Indian Pavilion.

Smoke is still poring from the wreckage and the aftermath is being watching by the thousands of holidaymakers.

(Photograph Phil Barker)

To the right of the Pier showing a different angle to the previous photograph.

In 1938 tragedy struck again as the second version of the Pavilion set on fire in June. Thus the venue closed again, but only for a year this time.

The second fire was thought to have started in a dressing room.

(Photograph Phil Barker)

Under the Pier itself, showing only the remaining iron structure left in place.

The design is a testament of engineer Eugenius Birch as he thought if they were constructed using wrought iron it would create issues if boats were to crash into them. Cast iron would be easier to repair, however.

(Photograph Phil Barker)

A stunning view that was taken from Blackpool Tower showing the smoke still billowing to the right of the Pavilion.

As the tide is drawing back, more crowds are beginning to appear to watch the aftermath of the damage that the fire caused.

(Photograph Phil Barker)

The Indian Pavilion still on fire.

This image taken from what is now the Comedy Carpet.

The tide appears to be going back out again and more people can be seen attempting to get a better look and get closer to the pier itself.

(Photograph by Steve Gomersall)

A personal photograph that was kindly loaned by Steve.

In the distance you can just about make out North Shore, but this shows up close the remaining parts of the pier and the havoc that the fire had caused to her.

(Photograph Phil Barker)

1921 to 1924 would be the date that this postcard would have been taken, as the pavilion has still not been rebuilt as can be seen to the far right of the image.

I love this old image as it shows how busy the pier was and the fashions of the day, when life moved at a gentler pace.

(Photograph Phil Barker)

This image I feel would have possibly been taken from the 'Clifton Hotel' due to the angle.

It was originally going to be the cover for this book.

What is interesting is all the 'little things' that can be seen within the image. The fashions of the day, the old car, the adverts for 'On with the Show' and the seafarers concert party times at the 3d entrance fee.

(Photograph Barry J Barnes)

A group shot of the young ladies that made up the 'Lawrence Wight Girls' who saw what a lucrative market was to be made writing and selling his own songs that could be used in stage shows of the era.

In this way his own compositions could be incorporated and therefore catering to the changing taste of the visiting masses of holidaymakers.

(Photograph Barry J Barnes)

In the middle is Barry's mother Barbara Taylor, who was around 15 when this photograph was taken of her when she was one of the Lawrence Wright Girls performing in shows on the North Pier.

Barry also informed me that 'She had joined the Annette Schultz girls when she left school at 14 and went on to join the Musical Elliotts in the late 1930s. Happy days!

(Photograph Barry J Barnes)

Another group shot that includes Barry's mother, Barbara Taylor. His mother later met her father in the resort in the late 1930's, marrying in 1941.

Barry's dad was Syd Barnes, and amongst other positions he was senior manager at the Pavillion, and then later at the Opera house in the Winter gardens.

Barry remembers his parents telling him what a great experience it was to perform in the resort in the late 1930's and they had many happy memories of that time.

(Photograph Phil Barker)

A lovely postcard showing the hustle and bustle of the day.

On the Pier we can see banners and flags advertising 'On with the Show', with a myriad of holidaymakers making their way about the promenade and walking through the entrance of North Pier.

Also on view is the information booth with one lady taking advantage of the shade with a strategically placed deckchair to soak up the Blackpool summer rays.

(Photograph Phil Barker)

Lawrence Wright (1888 to 1964) had a great love for Blackpool and the theatrics of the town so much that he lived in a house that looked like a castle, which had been built for a Mr. Arthur T. Knowles. Later this was bought by Lawrence (real name Horatio Nicholls). Running 'On with the Show' for over 30 years, he brought love, laughter and variety to the North Pier.

(Photograph Barry J Barnes)

There is no danger of knowing which show these lovely young ladies belong to!

Another wonderful photograph provided by Barry of his young mother 9th in from the right.

I love the way that all the girls are wearing one-piece 'outfits' with the LW logo on them.

(Photograph Juliette W Gregson – own collection. Iinformation Phil Barker)

1944 programme showing some of the popular stars of yesteryear, Dave Morris was an original comedian of the day, not at all hindered by his blindness; he actually incorporated it into his act. On the bill was the famous soprano, Sylvia Cecil who was known for singing musical comedy and a career that lasted over 50 years.

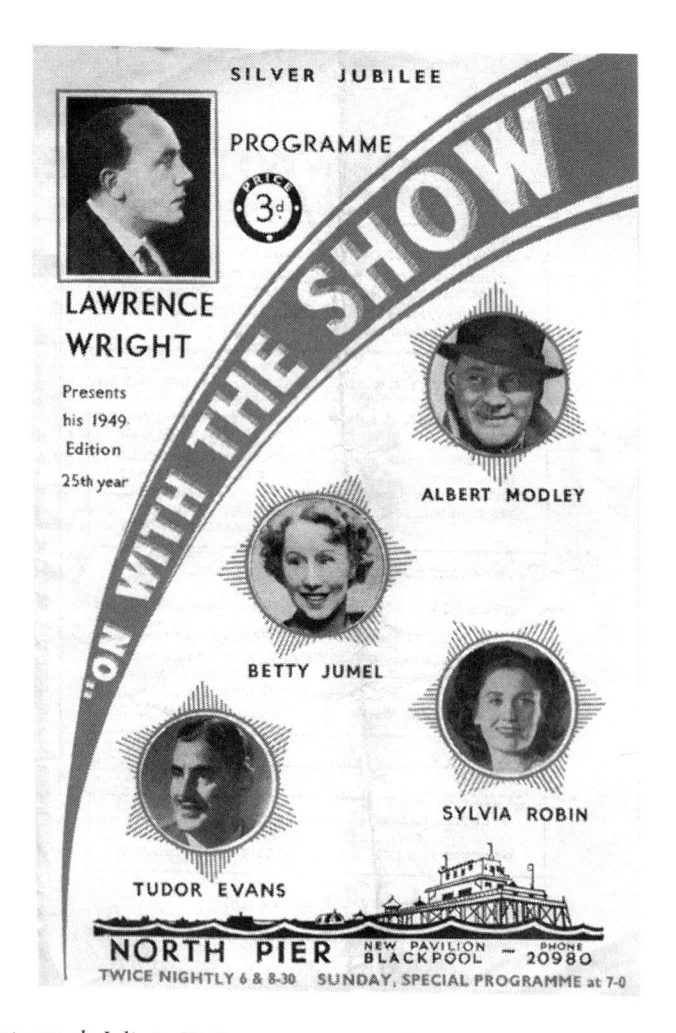

(Photograph Juliette W Gregson – own collection/information Phil Barker & Cyril Critchlow Collection - courtesy of Local & Family History Centre, Blackpool Central Library)

1949 programme showing a local Fylde coast talent Betty Jumel, who followed in her fathers (Harold Jumel) variety steps. Tudor Evans a well-known and versatile baritone was also on the bill that year. Albert Modley was providing comedic interludes that included his notorious catchphrase, 'Isn't it grand when you're daft.' I have used this line a few times never realising the history and man behind it!

(Photograph Peter Lindup)

Teresa Mary 'Tessie O Shea was incredibly popular in Blackpool during the 1930's

Very much know for her versatility, she played on her 'weight' and was known by her song, 'Two Ton Tessie from Tennessee'. Bertram Harry Gutsell, Bertini's real name was one of the most successful bandleaders or the era, who went from strength to strength by just catering for the masses with his 'band' music to dance to.

(Photograph Juliette W Gregson – own collection)

A 1953 programme with Lawrence Wright using the 'Queens' coronation events to show patriotism to the crown and of course this would appeal to the visitors from London and surrounding area's.

Stars of the day included 'The Beverley Sisters', 'Jack Storey, 'Phillip Kelly' and the 'Tiller Girls'.

On a Sunday at 7.45 Lawrence Wright changed the running and created an entirely different programme, again to entice a return visit!

(Photograph courtesy of Local & Family History Centre, Blackpool Central Library)

Taken looking towards the pavilion, a marvellous shot of the patrons leaving Lawrence Wrights 'On With the Show'.

I adore the way that the Pier looks so busy with all the people of the day wearing what seems to be their 'Sunday best' clothes.

LADY OF THE FAN,
IN LAWRENCE WRIGHTS "ON WITH THE SHOW," NORTH PIER, BLACKPOOL.

(Photograph Phil Barker)

Lady of the fan 1938 postcard showing the lengths Lawrence Wright put into making his shows such a success.

Even though this is a postcard you can see the intricate detail of the stage set and the precision that the costume designers had to work to.

(Photograph Phil Barker)

The front cover of the 1902 North Pier programme that was later used as a postcard.

It shows the original Pavilion before it was destroyed by the fire in 1921. The middle drawing shows the intricate ironwork of the Band Stand and surrounding shops and café.

The final illustration shows an aerial shot of the majestic ness of North Pier herself.

(Photograph Phil Barker)

An excellent advert of the era showing all the wonderful Blackpool Tourist attractions of the day.

We can see Blackpool Tower, Big Wheel, Winter Gardens, all three Piers and much more.

I quite like the way the creator took artistic license with the size of one the steamers. It looks like it was as long as North Pier!

Blackpool North Pier

BLACKPOOL OF THE FUTURE.

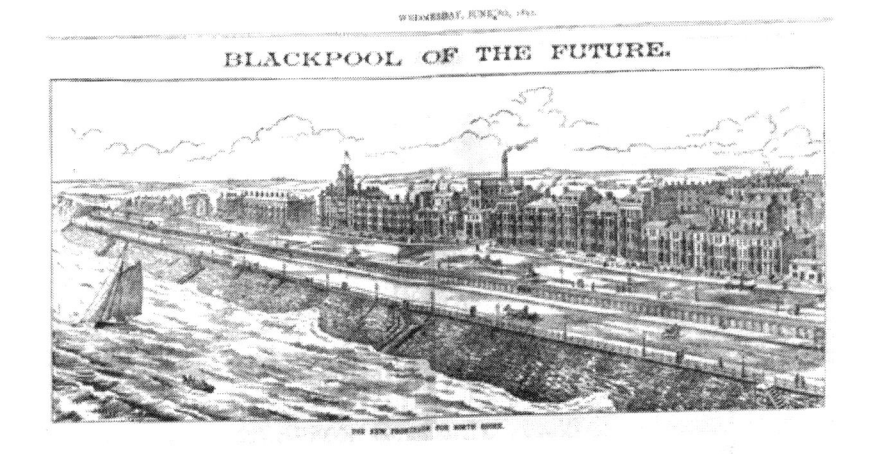

(Photograph Phil Barker)

An 1892 paper clipping of Blackpool of the future, showing the new promenade for North Shore.

Elements of the building in this clipping are still around today and can be seen looking from the Pavilion end of the North Pier.

Alas we no longer have the enclosed front terraced gardens as they have now been given over to road widening and car parking.

> **NORTH PIER, BLACKPOOL.**
> The Finest Pier in Europe.
> *Magnificent New Entrance and Arcade.*
>
> *Daily Programme—Season 1903.*
>
> OPEN-AIR **Promenade Concerts**
> — BY —
> MONS. SPEELMAN'S Splendid Orchestral Band.
> At 10-30 a.m. and 7-30 p.m.
>
> *Entertainments*
> At 3-0 and 7-45 p.m.
>
> EASTER WEEK, and every FRIDAY, SATURDAY, and MONDAY, from the 10th JULY, at 7-30.
> GRAND **Special CONCERTS**
> In the INDIAN PAVILION,
> At which the Leading Artistes of the Day will appear.
> ✱ FULL BAND ✱
> Conductor and Solo Violin · Mons. SPEELMAN.
>
> FLEET OF STEAMERS.
>
> Admission to Pier and Open-Air Promenade Concerts ... 2d.
> Annual Tickets ... £1 1s.
> Weekly Tickets ... 1s. and 2s. 6d
> Week-End Tickets ... 1s 6d

(Photograph Phil Barker)

Blackpool North Pier was no stranger to self-promotion as this 1903 programme shows, boasting 'The Finest Pier in Europe'!

A full day of events is on offer, with bands and entertainments to cater for all tastes and budgets, as can be seen by the prices for daily, weekly and annual tickets.

Also to tempt, a 'Fleet of Steamers' enabled visitors to travel and explore the sea and North West.

(Photograph Phil Barker)

Another North Pier programme, which was produced in colour at the time of print by Maxwell & Co printers. Some of the deigns produced are held in the Victoria and Albert Museum in London. We are very lucky that the museum now conserves art and design that has such a place in the heritage of Blackpool's North Pier

(Photograph Phil Barker)

Chiefs in charge of Blackpool's regeneration may have seen this advert describing her as 'Britain's Playground', as more recent developments in the town have been named the 'People's Playground. In 2009 many national newspapers reported that 'Hitler' had spared the resort and had said not to bomb or destroy the Tower or any of the three piers as he had intended on making Blackpool his headquarters.

Blackpool North Pier

(Photograph Phil Barker)

I love this view of Blackpool showing an alternative view of the town.

Peeking to the right, we can see the North Pier. The painting also includes a stark perspective of two iconic buildings, one being the cenotaph. The inscription reads "In Memory of Our Glorious Dead, 1914-1918, 1939-1945".

Every year The National Veteran's Day commemorates the lives of those lost in the wars.

(Photograph Phil Barker)

A rather abstract advertisement for Blackpool and the North Pier that reminds me of the style of the 'Art Deco' period which examples of which can be seen round the town.

This image seems to just show the enjoyment a simple walk down the Pier can create.

(Photograph Phil Barker)

Every year the tourism department produced a 'Holiday Journal'.

In this one, a lovely lady is beckoning you invitingly to visit Blackpool.

All the major attractions had a 'write up' stating prices and when open for business, North Pier was no exception and had a one page advert in this edition.

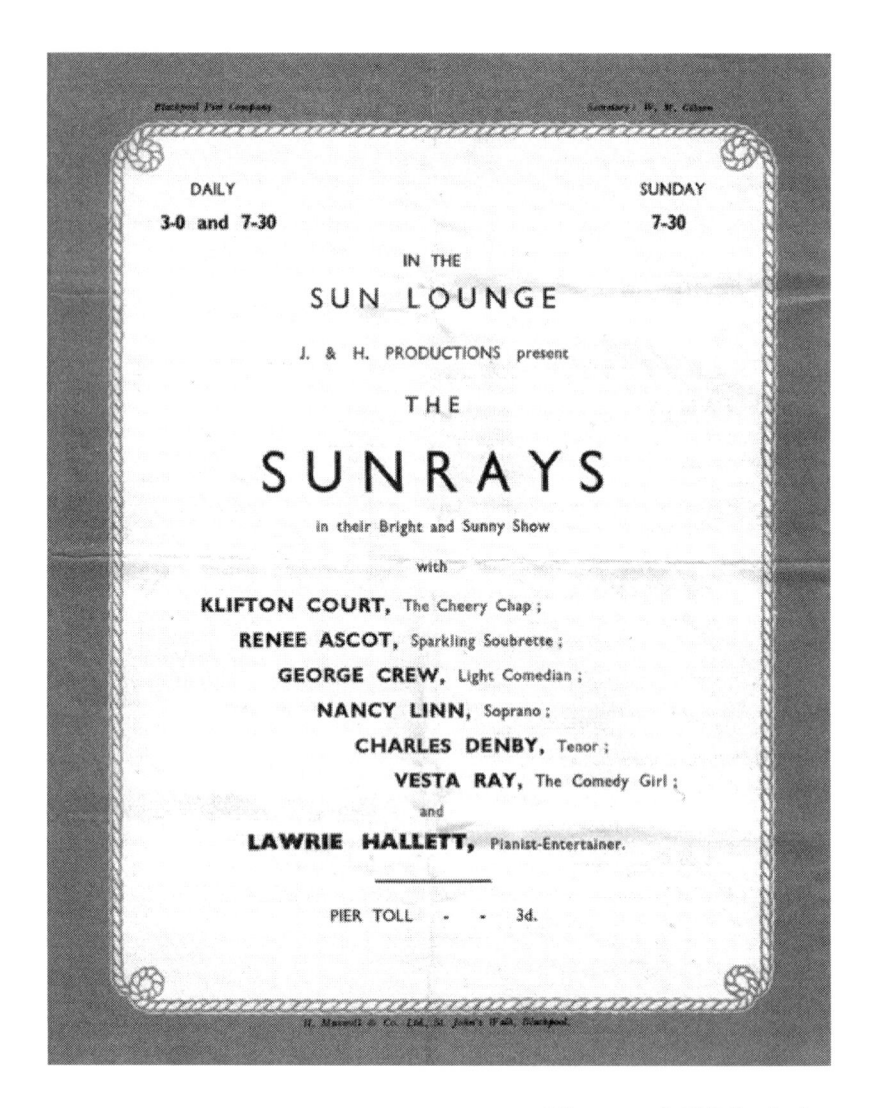

> DAILY
> 3-0 and 7-30
>
> SUNDAY
> 7-30
>
> IN THE
>
> ## SUN LOUNGE
>
> J. & H. PRODUCTIONS present
>
> THE
>
> # SUNRAYS
>
> in their Bright and Sunny Show
>
> with
>
> **KLIFTON COURT,** The Cheery Chap ;
>
> **RENEE ASCOT,** Sparkling Soubrette ;
>
> **GEORGE CREW,** Light Comedian ;
>
> **NANCY LINN,** Soprano ;
>
> **CHARLES DENBY,** Tenor ;
>
> **VESTA RAY,** The Comedy Girl ;
>
> and
>
> **LAWRIE HALLETT,** Pianist-Entertainer.
>
> PIER TOLL - - 3d.

(Photograph Phil Barker)

A delightful programme showing what's going on in the Sun Lounge. The price for what would have been a very enjoyable afternoon was 3d. After asking my Dad what this was, he explained it was a three-penny bit, which he thought was about 3-5 pence in today's money. Quite a good price for an afternoon of quality entertainment.

(Photograph Juliette W Gregson – own collection)

Frank Randle (born Arthur McEvoy) was what we would class today as an alternative comedian. His genre – he just appealed to the common masses. If history is to be believed he would at times refuse to appear in shows due to being intoxicated. The paying fans would forgive him happily accepting a refund and waiting until he appeared again!

(Photograph Juliette W Gregson – own collection)

On Saturday 7th July 2012 I was lucky enough to be invited to an event for the Frank Randle Appreciation Society. Every year they hold an annual event to celebrate Frank Randle's life and liver - Music, Film and Fun organised by the Cuthbert Club. The plaque was officially opened on the 7th of July 2007, and is situated on North Pier where Frank performed in many shows opposite the Carousel Bar. (Quite fitting if you believe how much he could drink!)

(Photograph Juliette W Gregson – own collection)

After watching three films 'Bella's Birthday', 'Full House' and 'Randle and All That', I was given the opportunity to chat to the group.

I was given a history lesson in Frank's connection with Blackpool and the North Pier, which, shall we say, was quite an eye opener.

However, I will be attending the 2013 reunion!

Standing in front of the plaque is Michael Leader, founder member of the Laurel & Hardy Appreciation Society and 'Eastenders' milkman, very much a font of knowledge!

(Photograph Juliette W Gregson – own collection)

Sooty is now owned by the brilliant Richard Cadell, who bought the rights on Sooty's 60th anniversary from the Corbett family.

We all know the history of how Harry Corbett discovered him on North Pier, and how his son Matthew carried on the tradition.

I wanted to recreate Sooty on the North Pier so took him down for the day (helped by my good friend Paul Rodgers!) and had immense fun just wandering up to people and tapping on the shoulder and waving!

(Photograph David W Gregson)

I had the fantastic chance to have a phone conversation with Matthew Corbett about his father Harry, Blackpool and his memories of the Pier and shows.

Matthew reminisced about the summer seasons in Blackpool and the 'Stars' that appeared in the resort, such as Shirley Bassey, Tommy Steele and Ronnie Ronalde.

He remembers staying at the 'Welbeck Hotel', and whilst on holiday with his parents and brother, being invited by Cliff Richard backstage as he wanted to chat to Harry.

Matthew was delighted that Cliff was such a fan and how kind he was about his dad.

(Photograph Peter Lindup)

A few familiar favourites adorn this 'On with the Show' programme.

Less well-known acts included Anita Martell, who was a talented female dancer and juggler of the era.

Sutherland Felce was a magic performer, who incorporated comedy quips as he went about his performance. Known for doing monologues he was very popular in London and was in great demand for 'summer seasons'.

NORTH PIER
ARCADE THEATRE

EASTER ATTRACTION

GOOD FRIDAY, SATURDAY and MONDAY
at 2-30 and 7-0 p.m.

SPECIAL MORNING SHOWS
SATURDAY and MONDAY at 11-0 a.m.

ERNEST COLCLOUGH presents

EASTER SERENADE

with Blackpool's Star Comedian

CHARLIE PARSONS

and

BRIAN MASSEY Your Favourite Singing Star	**IAN VINT** Columbia—T.V. Recording Voice
BETTY AUSTIN Songs You Love	**JAMIE NELSON** Country & Western
AL BOS The Happy Minstrel	**SUZANNE** Magical Moments
JOYCE TERRY Personality Plus	**ARTHUR AUSTIN** Musically Yours

AFTERNOON and EVENING — Reserved Seats 2/6. Children 1/3.
MORNING SHOWS — Admission 1/-. Children 6d.

SPECIAL SHOWS EASTER SUNDAY at 2-30 and 7-0 p.m.
Reserved Seats 2/6. Children 1/3.

MAXWELLS, BLACKPOOL

(Photograph Phil Barker)

Charlie Parsons was a firm favourite with the crowds at North Pier and had great seasons as a comedian in the resort.

He was also brilliant with the younger members of the audience, and would, at times, often invite them onstage to perform a 'turn' with him.

(Photograph Phil Barker)

Another example of an early North Pier show programme, not quite as exciting in design as in previous years, only showing the Pier herself and not advertising any of the supporting acts that were performing.

"SHOW TIME" AT THE NORTH PIER PAVILION

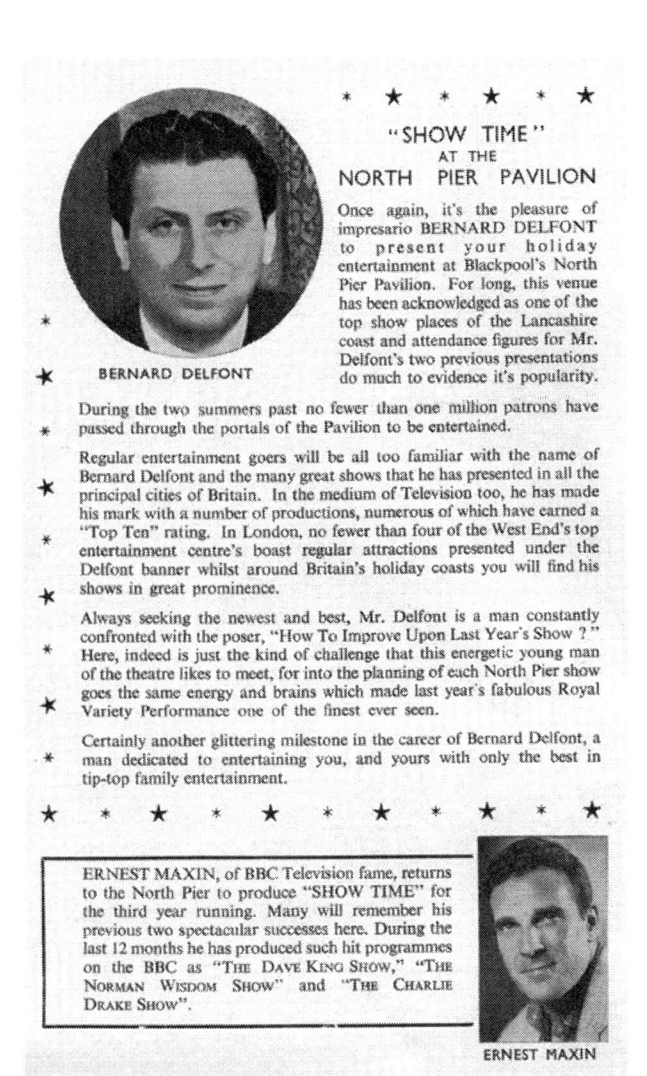

Once again, it's the pleasure of impresario BERNARD DELFONT to present your holiday entertainment at Blackpool's North Pier Pavilion. For long, this venue has been acknowledged as one of the top show places of the Lancashire coast and attendance figures for Mr. Delfont's two previous presentations do much to evidence it's popularity.

During the two summers past no fewer than one million patrons have passed through the portals of the Pavilion to be entertained.

Regular entertainment goers will be all too familiar with the name of Bernard Delfont and the many great shows that he has presented in all the principal cities of Britain. In the medium of Television too, he has made his mark with a number of productions, numerous of which have earned a "Top Ten" rating. In London, no fewer than four of the West End's top entertainment centre's boast regular attractions presented under the Delfont banner whilst around Britain's holiday coasts you will find his shows in great prominence.

Always seeking the newest and best, Mr. Delfont is a man constantly confronted with the poser, "How To Improve Upon Last Year's Show ?" Here, indeed is just the kind of challenge that this energetic young man of the theatre likes to meet, for into the planning of each North Pier show goes the same energy and brains which made last year's fabulous Royal Variety Performance one of the finest ever seen.

Certainly another glittering milestone in the career of Bernard Delfont, a man dedicated to entertaining you, and yours with only the best in tip-top family entertainment.

BERNARD DELFONT

ERNEST MAXIN, of BBC Television fame, returns to the North Pier to produce "SHOW TIME" for the third year running. Many will remember his previous two spectacular successes here. During the last 12 months he has produced such hit programmes on the BBC as "THE DAVE KING SHOW," "THE NORMAN WISDOM SHOW" and "THE CHARLIE DRAKE SHOW".

ERNEST MAXIN

(Photograph Juliette W Gregson – own collection)

Bernard Winogradsky arrived with his parents and brother as a Russian/Jewish emigrant before WW1 had started and settled in London. Later using the stage name 'Delfont' he had a vision of excellence and brought about the change in seaside shows and many more in the resort. Known for his vibrant 'Show Time' productions on North Pier Delfont raised the bar for the rest of the resort.

BERNARD DELFONT Presents

Showtime

NORTH PIER PAVILION BLACKPOOL

(Photograph Juliette W Gregson – own collection)

Des O'Connor could always be relied upon to provide good quality family entertainment, and was one of the headliners in this 1966 programme. His introduction in the programme is quite interesting to say the least! 'Des O'Connor, good looking with hazel eyes was born in London. He joined the Royal Air Force and was forced into a talent competition, because he was always clowning around when he should have been working. He won first prize £5!'

(Photograph Juliette W Gregson – own collection)

A 1977 'Delfont Showtime' programme that had a wealth of 'stars' that year, such as Syd Little & Eddie Large who got their breakthrough on 'Hughie Green's Opportunity Knocks, Syd to this day still lives in the Fylde coast.

Frank Carson was another star who loved the town so much he had a house in Blackpool, Layton and was always to be seen about the town. Ever the gentleman, sadly he died in February 2012, a great loss to variety and Blackpool.

(Photograph Phil Barker)

A 1968 programme that shows Mike & Bernie's Showtime. For years, I must admit, until doing research for this book, I thought that only Bernie did shows with his adorable dog 'Schnorbitz', not realising he had a brother. The brothers were very successful and had their own show that ran between 1965 and 1973, until family matters erupted and they never worked together again.

(Photograph Juliette W Gregson – own collection/information kindly provided by Nick Entwistle)

Here we have a 1930's streamlined double-decker tram advertising Russ Abbot on North Pier, as seen travelling towards town and just about to pass 'Cocker Square'.

It was one of two rebuilt in the early 1980's with new electrical equipment and a front entrance for one-man operation.

Although a rebuild of an old tram, it's classed as the ultimate development of a traditional British double-decker tram.

It's now preserved at the National Tramway Museum at Crich.

(Photograph Graham Coleman)

In 2004 Blackpool North Pier was graced with an exhibition of George Formby items that would have marked his 100th birthday.

A firm favourite with all, the event was opened by the younger brother of George, Ted, who was 87 at the time and was delighted that Blackpool and the North Pier had been able to host the event that showcased many never seen before photographs and assorted items of memorabilia.

(Photograph Andi Musson)

North Pier had always welcomed performers and stars of the day, and in more recent years this has been quite apparent.

Here Andi Musson meets one of his idols 'Sinitta' during a Blackpool Pride event, held on the Pier in 2011.

Andi remembers that even though she was on crutches at the time, she was lovely when asked for pictures and cd's to be signed on his behalf.

(Photograph Juliette W Gregson – own collection)

North Pier has never been afraid to keep moving with the times and 'bang up to date' with the latest trends.

Here, in June 2012, I was invited to take photographs for the 'Summer Soiree'. These are the talented 'Freefly Crew', who are just simply amazing, as you can see by the image!

(Photograph John Burke)

The first official "Miss Blackpool" beauty contest was won by Elaine Smith (not the Civic Trust Elaine!) and was originally held at South Shore Baths, then later at North Pier.

The town went on to host the finals of the Miss United Kingdom from 1958.

Sporadic beauty contests for a "Miss Blackpool" crown had been held during the 20s and 30s.

Here we have the beauty contest line-up, North Pier Sun Lounge, Blackpool May 1982.

(Photograph John Burke)

Raymond Wallbank was the resident organist an the North Pier Sun lounge from 1965 to 1995, spanning an impressive career catering to the crowds that loved his music.

Raymond took great pride in being a key fixture and can be seen here comparing the 1982 Beauty Show.

(Photograph John Burke)

Raymond at the organ. This is how I remember him, as I was lucky enough to be taken to listen to some of his performances by my father David W Gregson (who was also a session organist that admired his versatility).

David also mentioned that he had a shop in Ansdell, Lytham and ran the successful Raymond Wallbank Organ Club.

(Photograph John Burke)

Various heats were held over the summer season and this 'Miss Blackpool Heat' was in June 1982. Alas I do not know the name of the lovely lady here, but admire anyone that can get up on a stage in a swimming costume in front of complete strangers!

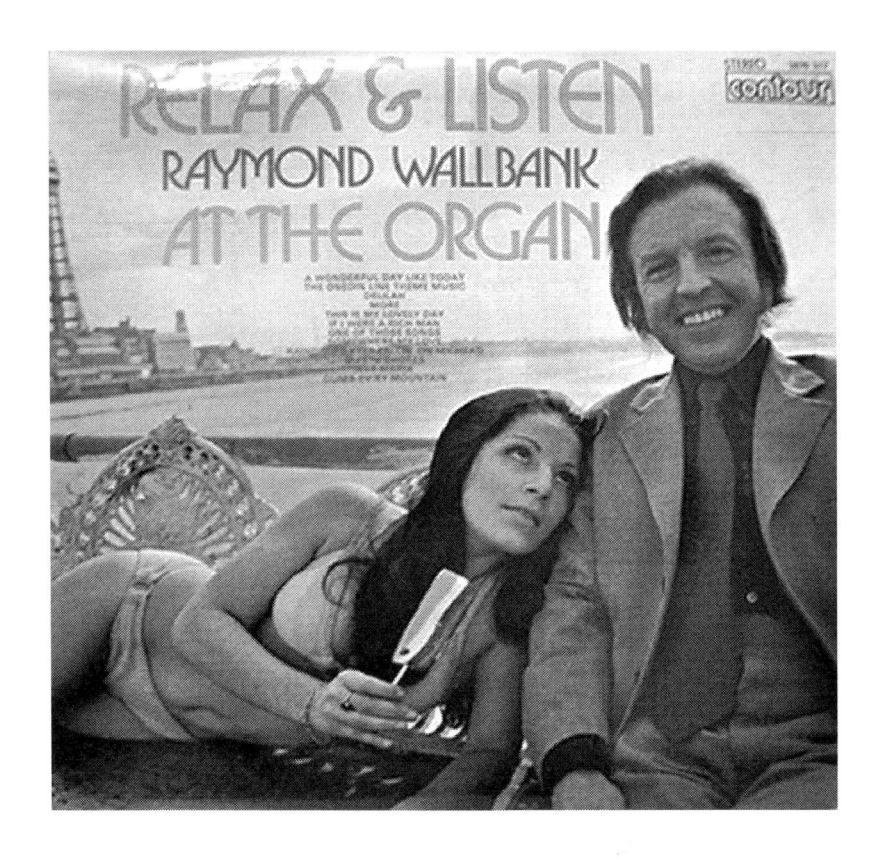

(Photograph Juliette W Gregson – own collection/Album David W Gregson)

My father was a great fan of Raymond Wallbank, and here we have one example of the many albums that he produced in his long spanning career.

We shall not see such a lovely gentleman of this calibre again as Raymond. He sadly passed away in Ansdell, Lytham in February 2010.

(Photograph John Burke)

A Miss Blackpool Heat in May 1982 that was being judged by the 1980 Olympic Ice Skating winner Robin Cousins.

No stranger to Blackpool, Robin had ice skated at the Blackpool Ice Drome in the early 1980's, and was always in great demand in the resort.

I also quite like the way that one of the gentlemen in the deckchairs seems to have fallen asleep!

(Photograph John Burke)

Here we have the 1982 Miss Blackpool Heat winner from May 1982. Judge, skater Robin Cousins, hands a cheque to Wendy Phizacklea, who looks absolutely delighted to have got first prize, or maybe because Robin was the judge on that day! It's nice to see the lady in the background as well who also seems to have enjoyed watching the parade.

(Photograph John Burke)

Blackpool has always had a long tradition of holding air shows in the town.

In more recent times we have been lucky to have them more or less every year.

Evoking memories of a bygone time, we see a flypast by a vintage 'Spitfire' that just about to pass over North Pier in 1985.

(Photograph John Burke)

In 1947 the first display by the RAF Aerobatic Team (now called the Red Arrows) took place at Squires Gate Airport in July.

It was organised by the Lancashire Aircraft Company.

The Red arrows are always in demand, but are regular visitors to Blackpool.

Here, from the busy beach, we can see them pass over North Pier in 2006.

(Photograph John Burke)

Another shot from 2006, showing the formation team flying very low over North Pier.

Watching with excitement was the vast crowd stood on the decking to watch the show.

A little known fact is that, in 2009, Flight Lieutenant Kirsty Stewart made aviation history when she became the first woman in the Red Arrows' aerobatic display team.

(Photograph John Burke)

In later years, as the need was no longer there for pleasure cruise trips, the jetty was altered for use as a helicopter pad used to operate short flights around Blackpool.

Here we have the helicopter on the pad in August 1991, just before take off. Storms in 1997, however, put an end to this and they obliterated the jetty that included the helipad.

(Photograph Juliette W Gregson – own collection)

As a regular visitor to the Blackpool Air Shows, I always try and get a good spot on the beach to watch the events unfold.

This was taken in 2010 after the show had finished and all the smoke from the display was drifting around and under the North Pier.

Even though this was taken during the day it's quite ethereal and just a little spooky.

(Photograph Ian McLoughlin Collection)

A favourite haunt for many photographers, including myself, is the 'underbelly' of North Pier.

Here, taken by Ian in June 1975, not much has changed at all, with the intricate yet study construction that Birch created so many years ago.

(Photograph Juliette W Gregson – own collection)

Taken in 2012 just near where the jetty would have been at high tide, showing some of the intricate ironwork that went into making what North Pier is today.

The North Pier has been awarded by English Heritage status as a Grade II listed building, due to it being the oldest surviving pier created by Eugenius Birch.

(Photograph Juliette W Gregson – own collection)

A June 2012 shot, where I managed to get a day when it was not raining to retry and recreate postcard shots of the North Pier.

Here at high tide we can still see some familiar landmarks, such as the Cenotaph, Metropole, Sacred Heart Church and the beginning of Queen Street

(Photograph Juliette W Gregson – own collection)

A 2012 photograph of some of the intricate ironwork to be seen in the 'Sun Lounge' at North Pier.

If you take the time to stroll around this hidden gem you will see many more fine examples that can be discovered just beyond the Carousel Bar. Since this was taken the bad weather of early 2014, a lot of damage has occurred to the structure.

(Photograph Roy Thomson)

Just before sunset round about October every year, a natural event takes place right before our eyes.

Migrating starlings gather, almost resembling a huge black cloud as they swirl and change direction over North Pier.

Over the years I have just gone to sit and watch this 'free show' as many others have as well to marvel at Mother Nature.

(Photograph Juliette W Gregson – own collection)

Taken just after the August 2012 Air show, I wanted to capture the symmetry of Birch's designs at low tide as I did not have any up to date photographs!

Many photographers have used this spot to capture images for personnel use, calendars and student film projects.

(Photograph Juliette W Gregson – own collection)

Taken in June 2012 just near the old sea wall defences underneath the main entrance, which are still in sight at low tide.

I was quite surprised at the amount of odd items that were attached to the structure itself, the weirdest being a bright orange teddy bear (a possible Blackpool Football club connection)!

(Photograph Juliette W Gregson – own collection/information Nick Moore)

Taken in July 2012.

I was standing halfway under North Pier to investigate how the structure held up under the duress of the weather.

The Pier rests on cast iron columns on the screw piles that are sunk into the seabed.

Apparently this was only the second pier that had been created using this ingenious method.

(Photograph Juliette W Gregson – own collection)

Taken in July 2012.

I then stood under one of the kiosks and was again amazed of the workmanship that must have gone into building and constructing North Pier.

Again seen here are the cast iron screw piles that are supporting iron girders, and of course the wooden deck of the pier.

How many feet have traversed below and above over the years?

(Photograph Juliette W Gregson – own collection)

Taken in August 2012.

I was walking my German shepherd/Rottweiler cross 'Christo' as she loves a good run across the beach.

Sitting (believe me this took a while as she would not sit still) just below where the lower jetty started, even at low tide there was still water and quicksand around the area.

(Photograph Juliette W Gregson – own collection)

Walking further out onto the beach, I went to the spot where the now long-demolished jetty would have ended.

To the left we can see the third version of the imposing 'Pavilion Theatre'; to the right the beautiful 'Sun Lounge'; and just in the centre a lone angler (he may have to wait a while for the tide to bring back the fish).

(Photograph John Burke/information Nick Entwistle)

Taken in 1982 showing a 703 'Balloon' tram that got its name from looking rather like an air ship.

This tram was said to be haunted, and the bell used to ring on its own!

A little known fact is that included in the corporation tramway by-laws, is the rule that tram queues at North Pier must not block ingress and egress from the Pier.

(Photograph Juliette W Gregson – own collection)

Blackpool's original tramway system dates back to February 1885, and is believed to be one of the oldest working electric tramways in the world today.

North Pier played a key destination for the visitors, having three short tracks that allowed ease of movement during peak times in the season and the illuminations.

(Photograph John Burke/information Nick Entwistle)

Tram '606', known as an 'Open Boat', was built by English Electric at Preston in 1934.

The driver in this photograph is called David.

Nick tells me that his nickname was 'Depot Cat', because he was never away from work, as can be seen here outside the North Pier.

(Photograph Phil Barker/information Nick Entwistle)

In 1991 North Pier installed their own tramway.

The engineers responsible for this delight were 'Harry Steer Engineering of Breaston'.

Able to hold up to 56 passengers, this provided a welcome addition to the pier facilities, especially as Blackpool's weather at times can be quite unpredictable.

(Photograph John Burke)

Taken in 1998, many people like to ride the tram to the end of the pier.

This proved very popular in the evening (depending on the weather) as theatregoers would make their way to the shows.

The driver was meant to collect the fair at the end of the short journey, but some (yes I was one!) would forget to pay.

(Photograph Roy Thomson/information Nick Entwistle)

The tram in question here used a diesel engine, which was quite costly to run and maintain.

Three smaller cars can be seen in this slide that were connected together to form the main vehicle.

North Pier had to having the decking reinforced to support the weight of this delightful train.

(Photograph Juliette W Gregson – own collection/information Nick Entwistle)

The tram ran from 1991 to 2004.

It was later removed, to be sold as scrap.

Whilst doing research for this book and speaking to owners, Peter & Sue Sedgwick, I was informed that there are future plans for the train to be reintroduced as part of their regenerations plans for the pier.

(Photograph Phil Barker)

An aerial view of the North Pier showing the beginning of the jetty, a very busy sun lounge and lots of holidaymakers just having a great day out.

Looking further into the background, the promenade below the Metropole is also incredibly busy with people, just strolling along on a Blackpool summer day.

(Photograph Phil Barker)

A lovely postcard showing the North Pier with jetty, and Talbot Square.

A lot of the landscape has now changed. By 1966 the Town hall spire had been removed as it was deemed to be unsafe.

One of the greatest losses was 'Yates Wine Lodge' in 2009, due to a fire started by an arsonist.

The iconic building was beyond repair and was pulled down.

(Photograph Juliette W Gregson – own collection)

Taken from the roof of Blackpool Superbowl (previously the 'Savoy Café') in 2011 at 8am in the morning, hence not a lot of people are walking along the Pier.

A stark contrast to earlier postcards that were produced by the Tourism department in bygone days.

(Photograph Juliette W Gregson – own collection)

As a supporter of Blackpool and her iconic heritage buildings, I purchased a Blackpool Tower Pass, which gave me access to sky views of the town.

This photograph taken in April 2012 shows a very quiet North Pier at low tide on a Friday morning.

(Photograph Martyn King)

Taken before 2009, as 'Yates Wine Lodge' is still situated at the heart of Talbot Square and the old sea walls are still in place.

Areas under the Pier are prone to quick sand, which can prove fatal for anyone.

Whilst taking the photographs for this book I came across just the one area that did this, which was where the lower jetty began.

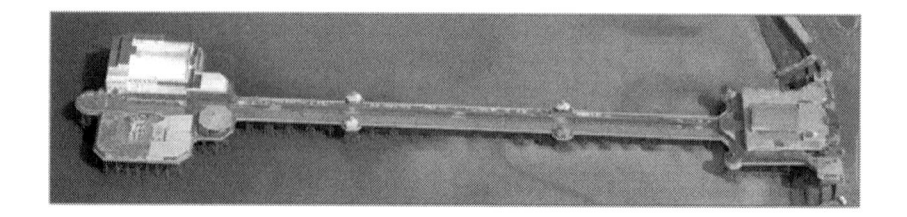

(Photograph Pete Skinner)

A brilliant aerial shot taken by Pete Skinner showing a 2012 view just as the tide is going back out again.

You can just make out in the sun lounge and the decking the deckchairs sitting waiting for people to come and sunbathe.

However during the year of 2012 we had more rain than shine, so little chance was had to catch the rays!

(Photograph David W Gregson)

A slide by my father in 1971, which, he remembers, was taken as he was strolling along the Pier with my mother.

A stark contrast of quite a calm day in reflection to an earlier image in the book (Image 25) that shows the jetty during a storm.

He recalls that the "Blackpool and Layton Angling Society" held an annual competition every year to see who could catch the most fish.

(Photograph Juliette W Gregson – own collection)

A postcard shot of North Pier taken from the 'Savoy Café' (now Superbowl – see Image 129 for a contrast from today).

Still showing the jetty before damage, and the tourist information booth where the 'Wedding Chapel' is now situated.

I am not quite sure what the castle building is near to the Pier, but think it could have been part of the illumination display.

(Photograph John Burke)

Another brilliant shot taken by John, which shows the jetty.

The jetty was actually added as long ago as 1866, and brought the North Pier's overall length to 1410 feet.

Such a shame that it was later destroyed by storm damage.

(Photograph John Burke)

I, and it seems John as well, enjoy going to the top of Blackpool Tower, even though we are both local.

Talking to friends and family, it's amazing how many actually have not had a visit in more recent years, especially after the company 'Merlin' have invested and brought the Tower to a magnificent level.

Taken from the top we can see the carousel has not been installed yet.

(Photograph Barry McCann)

Taken after the storm damage of 1997, Barry was walking along the beach taking shots of North Pier.

As you can see, there is a lot of damage to the jetty that, at the time, was thought to be too costly to repair.

(Photograph John Burke)

On Christmas Eve 1997, violent storms hit Blackpool with much damage being wrought.

The North Pier jetty was damaged beyond repair, this photograph being taken in June 1998 before the remaining detached section was demolished.

(Photograph John Burke)

Taken from central beach on a busy summer day, in the distance the damaged North Pier jetty.

The sea defences are not in place yet and many happy holidaymakers are just sitting back, enjoying the sun and sand.

Hopefully the tide was going out or the ice cream vans would have had to move pretty quick!

(Photograph Ashley Rolinson)

A more up to date 2012 image of the North Pier without the jetty, taken as the sun was just peaking behind the clouds before sunset.

A slow walk morning or late evening and you will catch many photographers getting iconic shots …

(Photograph Juliette W Gregson – own collection)

A more up to date, 2012 image of the end of North Pier, taken in June.

The 'anglers' still congregate at the end to fish, but after speaking to a few more mature members of the association they miss the loss of the jetty to fish from.

(Photograph John Burke)

Taken again by John at North Pier at dusk in September 1981.

The lights on the sun lounge and the pavilion have just been lit, giving the Pier a quite ethereal quality to the visitors and onlookers taking a stroll down the promenade.

(Photograph John Burke)

Taken in 1991, the carousel had just been installed on the North Pier using a 'Venetian' style two-tier design.

Unprotected against the sea elements, a decision was taken after the season to encase and wall around with glass and shutters, therefore protecting the structure from wind blown sand and sea spray.

(Photograph John Burke)

A closer photograph of the Venetian carousel.

It seems on inspection that the horses have feather dusters attached to their heads in place of a mane!

Also, one thing I never noticed is that there is a horse that's positioned at the top.

(Photograph Roy Thomson)

No 'Carousel' in this photograph provided by Roy, but still lots going on.

Deck chairs to the right are quickly filling up to get the best spot for sunbathing.

There's a North Pier gallery exhibition to be perused as well.

I wonder if they had any vintage images on show in the gallery that day.

(Photograph Juliette W Gregson – own collection)

A 2012 close up of the horses on the 'Venetian Carousel' (this time without the feather dusters in an earlier photograph).

I did actually go and have a 'twirl' on the ride itself, and must say I don't know why I didn't do this when I was in my younger days.

Beautifully crafted, I can see why this is such a popular attraction with young and old.

(Photograph Juliette W Gregson – own collection)

In the late 1960's, the old café was removed and the Carousel Bar built to cater for the changing taste in the clientele.

Here, a 2012 photograph shows the front entrance, in keeping with the theme of fun and old style carousel design.

(Photograph Juliette W Gregson – own collection)

Around the end of the 1930's, the earlier bandstand was removed and the sun lounge was erected in its place.

It's still there if you look in the Victorian style wrought iron canopy.

This photograph was taken after the 'Blackpool Gay Pride' event in May 2012.

(Photograph Juliette W Gregson – own collection)

Even though the sun lounge is exposed to the elements, this does not stop the entertainment and events from taking place.

This photograph was taken again at the 'Summer Soiree' in June 2012', and shows 'The Monster Squad' – a five piece funk, soul, hip-hop, rock and groove outfit.

Based in the North West they are fronted by singer songwriter Luke Gribbon, who you can see here wearing a rather fetching hat.

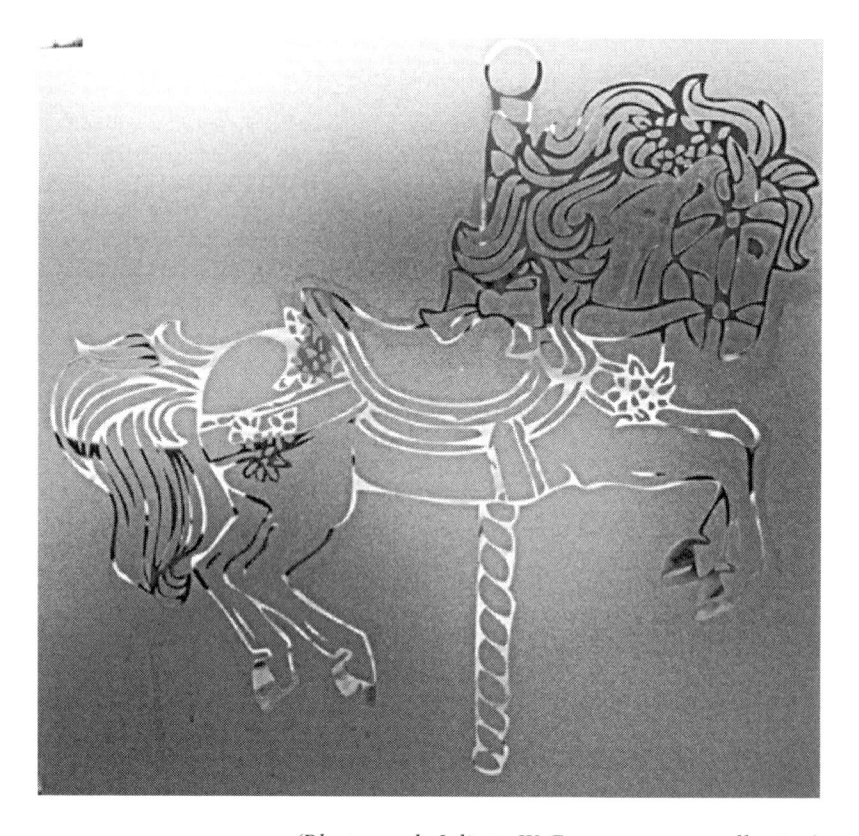

(Photograph Juliette W Gregson – own collection)

If you walk through the Carousel Bar towards the sun lounge outside, ponder a moment and look at the windows around you.

Embossed in frosted glass are the horses from the 'Venetian Carousel' in red white and blue decal.

Blackpool North Pier

(Photograph John Burke)

A very busy summer day taken in August 1996, showing how much the North Pier has evolved as the years have passed onwards.

No 'Carousel Bar or ride.

The train track has not been built yet for the tired and weary feet of the visitors, but you can just make out the sun lounge to the top left of the photograph.

(Photograph Juliette W Gregson – own collection)

Here in its third version we have the North Pier Theatre, just as you enter the bar area, before you go up the stairs inside for pre drinks and popcorn before your chosen show.

Just think of all the famous people that have stepped through the doors in all the years past.

If only walls could talk!

(Photograph Juliette W Gregson – own collection)

Taken in 2012, on the night of the 'Summer Soiree', as the evening went on the heavens opened again to the typical 'Blackpool' weather.

Escaping a while from watching the bands and entertainers I managed to capture a photograph showing the delight that even the North Pier can achieve during the rain.

(Photograph Juliette W Gregson – own collection)

A vast contrast to the two former pavilions, the 1939 version is still in use today, echoing the style of the 'Art Deco period'.

Fire nearly struck again, but was saved by the quick thinking actions of singer 'Vince Hill'.

He noticed that after leaving the theatre there seemed to be smoke emitting from the theatre and raised the alarm.

Therefore the fire services were in time to prevent any further damage.

(Photograph Juliette W Gregson – own collection)

The current capacity for today's theatre at a full house is 1500.

In more recent years, Stephen Mercer has been running 'Ghost Tours'.

They're worth a visit, as he explains: "Explore with us the interior of North Pier Theatre to see what really goes on when the cast and audience leave, the lights are switched off and the doors locked! Visit the haunted dressing room, learn of the Victorian lady, sit in the haunted seat in the theatre's auditorium and investigate the spooky storeroom."

(Photograph Juliette W Gregson – own collection)

The North Pier Theatre Bar just as you enter through the main doors.

It's worth a taking a little longer while sipping your drink to look around the Bar and see the vintage posters that adorn the wall, showing the Pier of bygone times.

(Photograph Juliette W Gregson – own collection)

Just before you go through the double doors to the North Pier auditorium you may spot this delightful wonder! This seems to be an old projector unit, that may or may not have been used in the theatre, alas I could not find out why and how it happened to be there!

(Photograph Juliette W Gregson – own collection)

Art Deco in design with the theatre windows, there is a running theme through the building itself.

If you look further around Blackpool and her heritage buildings you will see a lot of the 'half moon' deco designs in place, in the Tower, Winter Gardens to name a few.

(Photograph Juliette W Gregson – own collection)

Just outside of the main door of the North Pier Theatre, showing the lovely symmetry of the pillars and intricate designs from 1939.

Again, I was allowed by the family to take photographs when the Pier was closed, so it gave me a chance just to wander around with no visitors to admire the splendour of the building.

CLIFTON ARMS AND PIER HOTEL.
(Centre of Promenade and Opposite Pier.)

All Sitting, Dining, Drawing, Billiard, and Smoke Rooms face the Sea.

This old-established Hotel is replete with every convenience.

J. HARLING, Manager

(Photograph Phil Barker)

A marvellous advert showing the 'Clifton Arms & Pier Hotel'.

Just on show at the bottom is the beginning of the North Pier entrance, still with entrance gates that separated the classes that wished to frequent and stroll.

(Photograph Phil Barker)

A postcard looking towards Talbot Square in the background.

I love the way the younger ladies in this image are dressed with starched dresses and hats.

The gentlemen seem all to be wearing hats, as was the expected fashion and style of the era.

Very few men seem to wear hats today, possibly as they don't want to ruin their styled hair!

(Photograph Phil Barker)

There's such a lot going in this postcard.

The little pleasure boats are waiting for the tide to come in again, as the ladies are carefully walking down the steps to the beach.

We can see a few bathing huts that were pulled by horses. A little known fact was that men and women had separate huts and had to bathe at different times.

Women had to dress in an appropriate manner to 'prevent indecent exposure of the person'.

(Photograph Phil Barker)

A postcard of the 'sand express' railway, used only along this stretch of the promenade, moving sand from one end of Blackpool to the North side of town for future extension and expansion.

It only ran for a year but provided much needed employment for the area.

(Photograph Ian McLoughlin Collection)

In Ian's photograph here, we can see the visitors catching the sun's rays while watching the new 'Woolworth' building.

The building was finished and open in 1938, so I think this was possibly taken in 1937.

I have fond memories of going toy shopping, visiting the restaurant for cake, and of course buying sweets from the pick and mix selection.

(Photograph Phil Barker)

You can still see in this postcard the original gates that had a toll to enter North Pier.

Only in 2011 was the toll abolished for the general public. The new owners, Peter & Sue Sedgwick, wanted to bring back its Victorian heritage and therefore removed the admission price.

(Photograph Phil Barker)

An elegant postcard, which is more of a sketch or an etching of the hustle and tussle of the promenade and North Pier.

A long since gone age of dressing in your Sunday best, walking everywhere and looking quite elegant as you travel about in your 'barouche'.

(Photograph John Burke)

Taken in 1976, we can just see the old front façade of North Pier, which is nearly obscured by the old tourist information booth opposite Blackpool Tower.

How odd it looks with no comedy carpet or new sea defences, but this photograph gives you some idea of how close the road was to the sea!

To the right we can also see one of my childhood shops from which I loved to buy 'Sindy' items, Lewis's.

(Photograph Roy Thomson)

An atmospheric slide taken in 1989, showing, in the distance, a banner advertising the 'Russ Abbot Show'.

When you think how high the decking is on North Pier and look at the height of the waves crashing towards the shore, its no surprise there are not a lot of visitors promenading

(Photograph John Burke)

This photograph was taken in 1991, while work was being done on the North Pier decking in preparation for the laying of the tram track.

This would enable the visitors of the day, to travel from one end of the Pier to the other.

It was a great idea by the owners, as it would help the less mobile to reach the end and pop into the theatre to see the shows of the day.

(Photograph John Burke)

Taken in June 2008, John's photograph shows the old sea wall defences to the left, which have endured over 100 years of wear and tear to the elements.

Building was undertaken on low tides.

This image taken from the North Pier shows how much land was to be reclaimed back from the sea.

Ultimately the new stretch gained the name 'People's Playground' as each section of the headlands created was to be used for different activities.

(Photograph Juliette W Gregson – own collection)

Lots going on in this 2010 photograph, not least of which is the Comedy Carpet, created by Gordon Young, who I had the delight to chat to about his creation.

Taken from Blackpool Tower we can see the work about to begin where the 'dune grass' is to appear later in 2011.

The Wedding Chapel, just in shot, had recently been completed and, having visited, I can say it gives a great, uninterrupted view of North Pier.

(Photograph Juliette W Gregson – own collection)

Inside the Pavilion Theatre after backstage had been revamped because the previous owners had not kept this up to date.

Current owners Peter and Sue Sedgwick have, since buying North Pier in 2011, been updating and 'keeping the heritage of the pier'. The vision they both share is for restoration and redecoration also to bring back out the 'Victoriana'.

(Photograph Juliette W Gregson – own collection)

I have been lucky enough to be allowed to visit the North Pier by the owners, Peter and Sue Sedgwick, whenever I needed to acquire up to date photographs.

I particularly enjoyed capturing different times of the day and night, and the varied weather that the Fylde coast produces, as can be seen with this image.

(Photograph Juliette W Gregson – own collection)

On the 16th June 2012, Blackpool had a very famous singer perform – Elton John.

This photograph was taken the night before, showing the huge stage for his performance. The photograph was taken from North Pier.

Alas due to our unpredictable weather and the strong winds on the night the event at the Tower Festival Headland Arena, Elton's show was cut short.

(Photograph Juliette W Gregson – own collection)

Blackpool, of course, is famous for her illuminations, which in the year 2012 celebrated 100 years of the first display of light.

The Pier, naturally, has always joined in, and even on a rainy night the lights are indeed fantastic to behold.

I personally was lucky enough to be one of the centenary heads that were displayed opposite what was known as the Grade II listed Miners' Convalescent Home. I was also lucky enough on the 23rd of October 2013 to win a competition that allowed me to switch on the famous 'Blackpool illuminations'.

(Photograph Juliette W Gregson – own collection)

Over the years we have seen the North Pier grow in size, and have many different designs to the structures added to it.

When I look now at the current entrance to the arcade, and compare it with the original design, I can see how much has changed in the 150 years that North Pier has been running.

(Photograph Juliette W Gregson – own collection)

Most people forget the delights of what lies below a building or structure.

I was told as a young child to explore (and be careful) by my mother Kath M Gregson. "Look up and down," she said. "You never know what you will find."

I love the old marine life that just adds character to the North Pier.

(Photograph Juliette W Gregson)

On the very day, exactly 150 years after North Pier was opened, I was lucky enough to be invited to the 'Party' and had a most excellent time. Many local fans and civic dignitaries also enjoyed the free showcase and specially made North Pier sweets for the event.

(Photograph Juliette W Gregson – own collection)

The Sedgwick family cutting the 150th Birthday cake for the Pier – and yes it was lovely! We all got a goody bag from the event, which even had specially created North Pier Rock!

(Photograph Juliette W Gregson – own collection)

I feel that Blackpool has some of the most wonderful and beautiful sunsets, especially if you are standing on North Pier.
But I am biased!
On a final note, I thought this would be a fitting photograph to end the book about one of Blackpool's heritage gems, North Pier.

Blackpool North Pier

BIBLIOGRAPHY

http://www.itsahotun.com

http://www.blackpoolghostsphotography.co.uk

https://www.facebook.com/groups/blackpoolspast

http://www.rossallbeach.co.uk

Printed in Great Britain
by Amazon

TeX FOR SCIENTIFIC DOCUMENTATION